TABLE OF CONTENTS

EVERYTHING YOU NEED TO KNOW ABOUT

MEDICAL MALPRACTICE

IN PLAIN ENGLISH

WILLIAM A. CIRIGNANI, ESQ.

CIRIGNANI, HELLER & HARMAN
150 SOUTH WACKER DRIVE
SUITE 2600
CHICAGO, IL 60521

WWW.MEDSUIT.COM
WACINFO@CHHLAW.COM

WORD ASSOCIATION PUBLISHERS
www.wordassociation.com
1.800.827.7903

Printed in the United States of America.

ISBN: 978-1-63385-136-8

Designed and published by

Word Association Publishers
205 Fifth Avenue
Tarentum, Pennsylvania 15084

www.wordassociation.com
1.800.827.7903

INTRODUCTION

The fact that you're reading this book means you've likely experienced one of the worst events a human being can experience: injury or death of a loved one at the hands of someone in the medical profession. At Cirignani, Heller & Harman (CH&H), we know, of course, that any kind of death or serious injury is a horrible event, but when it is caused by the people who are supposed to heal us, it carries a special hurt. We know this because we've spent our careers meeting people like you. While it is pure arrogance to say we know exactly what you're going through, all of us here have experienced enough personal suffering and have walked along side enough people who have lost children, spouses, siblings, parents, and grandparents through medical malpractice to have developed a high degree of empathy for you.

There are two main reasons we wrote this book:

1. Unlike the few of us who do nothing but medical malpractice work, the average person knows nothing about what it is or how it works. In fact, the average lawyer doesn't even know. Even when more experienced lawyers try to explain this highly specialized area of

law, they use technical jargon that no one but a lawyer understands; we wanted to be different. We wanted to explain it in plain English. (We thought briefly of calling the book "Medical Malpractice for Dummies," but that name is trademarked and, frankly, not knowing about this area of law hardly makes someone a dummy.)

2. The odds are you found this book while looking for an attorney, and we're pretty confident that to get here you trekked through pages of lawyer advertising—advertising that gave you little or no help in finding the right lawyer for your case. Ads with lawyers holding fistfuls of cash that promise to kick insurance companies' butts or saying that they care about you more than all of the other attorneys combined are pretty useless when what you really need to know is something about what you are facing in bringing forth a medical malpractice case. It is a myth and a dangerous one to believe that all lawyers who advertise themselves as medical malpractice lawyers have the same ability and tools to handle your case. As you will learn, they don't.

In summary, we wrote this book to give you solid, reliable, and honest information that you can read in your own time to help you understand what medical malpractice law is all about. We think once you know exactly what you're dealing with you'll be armed to find the right lawyer before you actually hire one. Of course, if your case is one that meets our criteria, we would like you to hire us (more on why we're the right firm at the end of this book), but even if you don't, we're pretty confident that the choice you make will be a better one because of what you read here. By the way, if there is any place where we've failed at our task or any part you don't understand, let us know and we will fix that.

DISCLAIMERS

(the things our law firm is *not* legally responsible for)

This book is about general principles and is not specific legal advice to you, for you, or about your case. It is, in fact, impossible to give you or anyone legal advice until we talk to you directly and learn about what happened. So, until we meet, please use the book for its intended purpose: to teach you general principles about medical malpractice and not specific legal advice. Fair enough? And one more thing. Although this book was written by me (Bill Cirignani) and sometimes in the first person, please know that everything said in this book is believed by all of us, including our entire support staff. We all believe it passionately.

CHAPTER 1

WHAT THE HECK IS MEDICAL MALPRACTICE ANYWAY?

THE RULES OF THE PROFESSION

Next time you take your car to the mechanic, ask if there are rules or procedures in the profession regarding how to properly change oil, do a tune-up, or put your car onto the lift. Ask your hairdresser if there are rules about how to apply hair color. Ask your contractor whether building a wall requires knowing something about carpentry. If you drive, you can even ask yourself, are there rules of the road I am expected to follow whenever I get behind the wheel of my car?

Of course, the answer to all of these questions is yes. Rules apply to everyone (even lawyers) for all manner of tasks. So it is with nurses, doctors, hospitals, and every other caregiver, except that when we speak of the medical profession, we call the rules *standards of care*. But don't let this confuse you: standards of care are the rules the medical professionals must follow. Nothing more, nothing less.

Now, when a medical professional breaks the rules of the profession, it's called: *medical malpractice*. But because one term is never enough for lawyers, you may also hear terms such as *medical negligence, breaches of the standards of care, professional negligence*, or *professional malpractice*, but all of these terms refer to the same thing: breaking the rules of the profession.

THE TERM STANDARD OF CARE IS JUST ANOTHER NAME FOR THE RULE THAT MEDICAL PROFESSIONALS MUST FOLLOW. IF THEY DON'T, IT IS CALLED MALPRACTICE.

Some people ask if there is a rule book that contains all of the rules that nurses, doctors, and hospital are supposed to follow. The answer is no, because it would be impossible to have a written rule for every situation faced by a medical professional; however, the things taught in medical school, on the job, in research articles, in medical textbooks, at medical seminars, at professional meetings, and even by certain state and federal laws are all potential rules the medical profession must follow. The point is, just like the car mechanic, nurses, doctors, and hospitals cannot do what they do without learning and applying the rules of their profession.

DISCOVERING THE RULES

There are two primary ways lawyers discover the rules that apply in a given medical case: (1) researching the medicine and (2) consulting with medical experts. This is best seen by an illustration.

Many years ago the parents of a young girl who died of bacterial meningitis in the emergency department of a local hospital came to our office to discuss whether they had a medical malpractice case. Bacterial meningitis is an infection in the lining of the brain. It is a very serious medical condition. The parents told us that even though their daughter was very sick, she waited several hours in the emergency department before seeing a doctor and then several hours more before the doctor gave her any treatment.

Although we knew a lot about bacterial meningitis cases, the first thing we did was research the disease again because sometimes medical rules change over time. (Remember, the only rules that matter are the rules applicable at the time the injury occurred.) We discovered that treatment of bacterial meningitis hadn't changed in twenty years and that every possible source of information on the disease—medical textbooks, medical articles, seminars, and even the hospitals' own written policies—had the exact same rule: every patient suspected of having bacterial meningitis must get antibiotics as soon as possible, with the minimum time being no longer than an hour after the patient enters the hospital.

Because our clients' daughter didn't get antibiotics for eight hours, it was pretty obvious that someone—maybe the nurses, maybe the doctors, or maybe both—didn't follow the rules of the profession (that medical malpractice was committed). So we went to step two. We contacted a doctor specializing in emergency medicine and a nurse specializing in emergency department nursing and asked them to review our clients' daughter's medical records and tell us what they thought. After their review, they confirmed our suspicions: the medical personnel in the emergency department failed to follow the basic rules for treating bacterial meningitis. In summary, lawyers discover the rules of the medical profession by researching the medicine and talking to medical experts.

THE PARTS OF A LAWSUIT—WHY DO LAWSUITS TAKE SO DARN LONG?

A common question we get no matter the state in which we file a medical malpractice lawsuit is, how long will the suit take? The answer, and again it really doesn't matter which state we are talking about, is two to four years on average—sometimes longer, sometimes shorter. Why? There are two main reasons.

First, the people and institutions sued for medical malpractice are never in a rush to get things done. Ever. Some of this foot dragging is done strategically to harm your case. Defense lawyers and their clients know that memories lag, key witnesses die or move away, and plaintiffs (you) may get worn out by the process and quit or take *short money* the longer a lawsuit takes to resolve.

THE TERM SHORT MONEY MEANS TAKING A SETTLEMENT THAT IS SUBSTANTIALLY LESS THAN THE CASE IS WORTH. WE WILL DISCUSS SHORT MONEY AGAIN WHEN WE TALK ABOUT LAWYERS TO AVOID.

In fairness, some delay by the defense is innocent and a product of overworked defense lawyers with little time to do more than put out fires—that is, deal with the most pressing matters only. On the defense lawyer's side of things, there is tremendous competitive pressure to acquire and retain defense business so that most defense firms never say no to a new case regardless of their workload. Unlike quality plaintiffs' law firms that intentionally keep caseloads manageable, a defense firm rarely says no when an insurance company comes calling with a new case for it to handle. The defense firm knows that there are many, many lawyers out there who are happy to snap up any case they turn away. By taking on every case they're offered, however, defense firms become responsible for more work than they can handle, and the only way to get that work done is to delay doing it.

The second reason medical cases take so long is inherent in the way modern litigation works. Following are the parts of a lawsuit filed in Illinois:

WHILE THERE ARE VARYING RULES AMONG THE STATES, THE PRACTICE IN ILLINOIS IS VERY SIMILAR TO MOST.

THE LETTER OF MERIT

We will discuss tort "reform," and why I put the word *reform* in quotes, later in this book, but part of the recent laws dictating how medical malpractice lawsuits must be handled includes adding a *letter of merit.* Because the primary villain in medical malpractice lawsuits is believed to be the *frivolous lawsuit*—a lawsuit that has no merit—state legislatures around the country passed laws to prevent plaintiffs from filing a medical malpractice until they first receive a letter from a medical doctor who, after reviewing the medical records, will say that the lawsuit has merit—that is, who will say that the lawsuit is not frivolous.

A PLAINTIFF IS THE PERSON WHO WAS INJURED BY AND SUES THE MEDICAL PROVIDER. A DEFENDANT IS THE PERSON OR HOSPITAL THAT IS SUED.

Thus, before we can file a lawsuit in Illinois (and in many states), our firm must first get a letter of certification from a doctor who, after reviewing the medical records and case material, certifies that the lawsuit has merit. This part is simple for law firms with extensive experience in handling medical cases because they've handled medical malpractice cases for so many years that they generally know long before they send the case out for certification whether it has merit. Still, it is a part of the case that costs time and money and is therefore a *case expense.*

A CASE EXPENSE IS WHATEVER MONEY A LAWYER MUST SPEND TO MOVE A LAWSUIT FORWARD.

THE FILING AND SERVICE OF THE COMPLAINT, THEN THE ANSWER

With letter in hand, the next step is to draft, file, and serve the complaint. Like its name implies, a complaint is a document in which the complaints against the doctor, nurse, or hospital are written down and given to the defendants. In other words, the complaint contains a list of the rules that were broken by the defendants. The complaint need not contain every rule that was broken but enough so that the defendants know the gist of the complaints against them.

After the complaint is drafted, it gets filed with the court and then a copy must be given to each defendant. The technical name for giving a copy of the complaint to the defendants is *service*, and although there are rules about how exactly service must be done, it is a detail you do not have to know about. The point is, lawsuits start when the plaintiff files the complaint and gives a copy to the defendants.

Once the defendants get a copy of the complaint (or is served), he gets to "answer" it, which means they can admit that they broke the rules the way plaintiff says they did or they can deny that they broke the rules. Three guesses as to which of the two options is most often taken by the defendants. Correct. In 99.9 percent of the lawsuits filed, the defendants answer by denying that they did anything wrong.

After each defendant answers the complaint, the case moves into the most time-consuming stage of every lawsuit: the pretrial discovery stage.

PRETRIAL DISCOVERY

Generally speaking, *pretrial discovery* is the process by which each side asks the other side for information needed to prove its case at trial. For example, the plaintiff might ask for additional medical records, hospital policies and procedures, background on the defendant doctor, or details about what the doctor was thinking when care was provided. Conversely, the defendants might ask the plaintiff to produce all past medical records (to try to show that the plaintiff always had the injury and thus the defendants didn't cause it). Other things the defense might ask for would include details about what the doctor said or personal documents such as calendars and diaries.

As a plaintiff in a medical malpractice case, you will have to answer most of the questions posed by a defendant. All discovery is given under oath and must be complete and truthful. Let me say that again: all discovery is given under oath and must be complete and truthful. Now, I watch the *Good Wife* in which Chicago lawyers frequently bend the truth to help their case, and I have seen *Suits* in which New York lawyers always ignore the truth as if it were just an option on the table. I also know that some people think that these shows are examples of the kind of kick-ass lawyering that they need to find, but like all fiction, it's, well, fiction. Here is the truth: nothing hurts a legal case more than lying. Nothing. That is true for plaintiffs and defendants alike. So, never lie.

LYING HAS NO BUSINESS IN LITIGATION. I CANNOT EMPHASIZE THIS ENOUGH. DO NOT LIE.

TYPES OF PRETRIAL DISCOVERY

There are several different ways lawyers get the information they need for trial. Some of these discovery tools are arcane and apply only in weird cases involving wills or real estate. In medical cases, there are three primary ways of getting information: written questions (called *interrogatories*), requests to produce stuff, and depositions. Some examples follow of the first two types of discovery:

- Interrogatory: "State the name and last known address of every nurse who worked on 12/25/2010."
- Request to Produce: "Produce all of the photographs taken of plaintiff or his family."

Pretty basic stuff and, truth be told, these discovery devices rarely produce much of anything useful. I know, I know, there are exceptions, but most of the time these are routine discovery requests that produce routine information.

The third type of discovery, the deposition, is the mother of all discovery devices. It can make or break a case and is the single most important tool in the lawyer's tool bag, whether a plaintiff or defense lawyer. A deposition is the giving of live testimony under oath before trial. In a deposition, a witness (you, the doctor you're suing, or a hospital administrator, for example) is asked questions by the lawyers. Although very important, depositions usually take place in an informal setting such as a lawyer's conference room. Depositions must have a court reporter present to record everything that anyone says, which can then be printed later in what is called the *record* or *transcript*. The rule to remember in depositions is, with few exceptions, once something is said, it is said forever and cannot be changed. A deposition has three primary purposes.

First, it is the lawyer's opportunity to meet and evaluate a witness or a party. For example, a deposition reveals whether plaintiffs or defendants communicate well, whether they dress nicely and are attractive (I know, that is shallow, but it still matters), whether they argue defensively, whether they are easily angered, or whether they are arrogant. Ultimately, lawyers are trying to determine whether a jury will like and believe the witness (and right or wrong, those two characteristics go together).

Second, a lawyer takes a deposition to hear the story of what happened. It is the plaintiff's chance to explain his or her injuries or what the doctor said about the surgery, and it is the defendant's chance to explain what went wrong and why. Because medical records are impossible to read, incomplete, or just plain wrong, depositions may be the only way to get the truth about what happened.

Last, a deposition is an opportunity for a lawyer to get damaging admissions. In other words, it's a lawyer's chance to get you or a defendant to admit something that hurts you or the defendant's case. You may be wondering how anyone with half a brain would ever admit to something that hurts the case. Well, lawyers are generally not stupid. They've been trained to ask questions in a manner, or in an order, or in a way that doesn't make them look like admissions until they are. The truth is that many cases turn on the quality of the deposition. This is especially true when the witness is a doctor, nurse, and other intelligent and highly trained professional who may try to confuse the lawyer with technical medical answers. Thus, lawyers doing medical work not only need skill and experience to know what to ask and how to ask it but also need to know the significance of the answers they get.

While this description of depositions may scare you about the process, do not be afraid. If you hire a quality medical malpractice lawyer, you will get so prepared for your deposition that it will be like talking with your grandmother. Okay, not that easy, but close.

THE THREE STAGES OF DISCOVERY IN MEDICAL MALPRACTICE CASES

In most states, the discovery process in a medical case has three stages. In the first stage, most of the questions are directed to the parties only: the plaintiffs and the defendants. During the second stage, the parties will ask questions of all non-party witnesses, such as your family (who may know what happened or know how the injury has impacted your life), your treating doctors (who know details about your injuries), or any other nonparty witness (nurses, clerks, or anyone who has information about your case). The last stage is the expert stage. It is at this stage when the parties hire experts to testify in support of their case. If an emergency department nurse is being sued, for example, both sides will hire an emergency department nurse to testify in support of their case. In fact, with few exceptions, if the plaintiffs don't hire experts, they will lose the case without ever getting a single day in court. This is because the law requires an expert to explain the rules of medicine and how they were broken. No expert, no case.

Let's summarize:

- When nurses, doctors, or hospitals don't follow the rules of their profession, it is called medical malpractice.
- The rules are not written down anywhere, but they are taught and learned through school, research, articles, laws, and seminars.
- Lawyers find the rules through conducting medical research and by hiring experts.
- Lawsuits take a long time because the defense wants them to take a long time and because the discovery process takes a long time.
- The most important part of discovery is the depositions, which is where witnesses admit things that hurt their case.
- Plaintiffs must have experts or they lose.

Once the expert stage is done, the case is ready for trial. What a trial is deserves its own chapter, and it gets just that in Chapter 3. But first, we need to discuss the elephant in the room: Should I sue?

CHAPTER 2

SHOULD I SUE?

Because my law firm specializes in medical malpractice, I suppose the expected answer to the question of this chapter is, yes, of course you should sue your doctor, but that would be wrong. There is a lot of bad information about medical malpractice cases. Some think it's a get-rich-quick scheme, and sadly too many lawyer advertisements make it seem that way, but it is not. Others think medical malpractice cases are a scourge that must be stopped. These people pass laws that make it expensive or impossible to get justice. But those people are wrong, too. The right answer is that it depends. Following are some factors that might come up during your consideration.

TORT REFORM

Tort reform is a loaded term. You may not know what the word *tort* means, but you almost assuredly know that *reform* is supposed to mean stopping greedy trial lawyers, too many lawsuits, the courthouse lottery, the loss of jobs, the loss of doctors, the practice of defensive medicine, and the rising costs of medical care, among many other evils. I have no idea, of course, whether you believe these things are true, and when I started to write this section, I even thought about ignoring tort reform under the theory that no one would believe what a trial lawyer has to say on the topic anyway. But I ultimately concluded that ignoring it would be a mistake because, first, worrying about what impact a medical malpractice lawsuit has on the world around you is a credit to you and not a criticism, but to really consider the issue, you deserve to hear what both sides have to say and not just the political sound bites. I will help you do that.

THE TERM TORT IS THE TECHNICAL TERM TO DESCRIBE A WRONGFUL ACT THAT HURTS SOMEONE AND THAT THE LAW TRIES TO FIX. IT IS MUCH MORE THAN MEDICAL MALPRACTICE AND CAN INCLUDE EVENTS SUCH AS INJURY BY A CAR, STUFF FALLING FROM BUILDINGS, CONTAMINATED FOOD, OR DEFECTIVE CRIBS.

Second, I thought I could handle the credibility problem by citing only studies conducted by independent sources, sticking primarily with those published by the medical or business profession. The following data is taken straight from studies conducted by business professors, law school professors, doctors, or hospitals and were published in respected journals. So, please don't write off this section. Read the facts I cite, and if you want more information, such as the actual articles, e-mail me at wacinfo@medsuit.com, and I will send them immediately.

MEDICAL MALPRACTICE LAWSUITS ARE ABOUT GREEDY TRIAL LAWYERS, NOT GOOD MEDICAL CARE

It is a common belief that lawsuits are bad for our country and exist only to make lawyers rich. A recent study conducted by two business professors from Northwestern University tested this idea by examining the effects lawsuits have on deterring negligent behavior (rule-breaking actions). The study was designed to look at the quality of medical care after tort reform was enacted—that is, after there were laws to limit lawsuits. They used a commonly accepted measure of medical care quality called the Patient Safety Indicators (PSIs) that was developed by the Agency for Healthcare Research and Quality. Here are the results of the study:

> We find a gradual rise in rates for most PSIs after [caps were passed], consistent with a gradual relaxation of care, or failure to reinforce care standards over time. ... The decline is widespread, and applies both to aspects of care that are relatively likely to lead to a malpractice suit (e.g., ... foreign body left in during surgery), and aspects that are unlikely to do so (e.g., ... central-line associated bloodstream infection). The broad relaxation of care suggests that med mal liability provides "general deterrence" — an incentive to be careful in general—in addition to any specific deterrence it may provide for particular actions. ... We find evidence that reduced risk of med mal litigation, due to state adoption of damage caps, leads to higher rates of preventable adverse patient safety events in hospitals.

Pause and think about what you just read: laws passed to make it harder to sue medical care providers result in medical care getting worse. Of course, this outcome is just common sense. We all know that without accountability for careless behavior, many people—not all, but many—will continue being careless. Anesthesiologists are a good example of the positive benefit of accountability.

Anesthesiologists used to be sued all of the time and used to pay huge insurance premiums because when they hurt someone, they were usually hurt pretty bad. But instead of lobbying to change laws to make it harder to sue them, they asked themselves why so many people were getting hurt by their specialty. They analyzed the claims brought against them and quickly learned that there was much that they could do to improve patient safety. They then started implementing these changes, and today anesthesiologists own one of the highest safety ratings in medicine and pay some of the lowest insurance premiums. In 2002, the University of Michigan Health System did a similar thing: analyzed the lawsuits against its entities and developed safety changes from what it learned. The result? Lawsuits against its hospitals were cut in half, but more importantly, far fewer patients were getting injured.

What these studies prove is that by deterring careless conduct, medical malpractice lawsuits provide families with better medical care. Now, that is a good thing, isn't it?

MEDICAL MALPRACTICE LAWSUITS FORCE DOCTORS TO MOVE TO OTHER STATES

One often repeated argument to justify passing laws to make it harder to sue medical care providers is that doctors will move to states where there are such laws. In other words, doctors who fear lawsuits will desert your state for another unless you make it more difficult to sue them. On the surface, this makes some sense, but the research doesn't bear it out. *Chest Journal* is the official academic journal published by the American College of Chest Physicians. (In case you were wondering, "chest" doctors are doctors specializing in things such as lungs, intensive care, and sleep medicine.) In 2013, it published an article called, "Five Myths of Medical Malpractice." One of the myths it identified is about doctors moving because of malpractice laws: "Various researchers have studied the impact if damage caps on physician supply. They have found mixed evidence, suggesting that damage caps may have a small positive impact on physician supply in rural areas or particular specialties, but much less evidence of post-reform increases in statewide physician counts."

In fact, in states such as Texas, changes to the law made no difference—doctors weren't leaving before the reform, and their supply didn't increase after the reform.

In an extensive study conducted by two law school professors (Northwestern and University of Illinois), the authors found no correlation between reform and physician supply; that is, they found that risk of medical liability had nothing to do with where doctors practice. Instead, doctors worked in states where they grew up or went to medical school or where they otherwise wanted to live.

MEDICAL MALPRACTICE LAWSUITS FORCE DOCTORS TO ORDER TESTS PATIENTS DO NOT NEED (DEFENSIVE MEDICINE)

Defensive medicine is a funny phrase. In some respects all medicine should be defensive, meaning that if the goal of ordering tests is to rule out conditions or diseases that could kill us, then such medicine is a good thing. (For example, I went to the hospital with chest pain, and the doctor ordered tests to see if I was having a heart attack even though he thought it was most likely a muscle strain. That is a form of good defensive medicine.)

In reality, the defensive medicine that concerns people is the kind in which unnecessary tests are ordered solely to give the impression that everything that could be done was done in the event of a bad outcome and a lawsuit. Of course, no doctor should be ordering unnecessary tests because they are, by definition, unnecessary; however, sometimes fear can make even doctors do silly things. The question is whether the data—the evidence—shows that they are really doing this. The authors, including medical doctors, of a study published in the *New England Journal of Medicine* stated the problem this way: "Many believe that fear of malpractice lawsuits drives physicians to order otherwise unnecessary care and that legal reforms would reduce such wasteful spending. … We investigated whether these substantial reforms changed practice [in emergency departments].

The results of their study were a resounding no: "Legislation that substantially changed the malpractice standard for emergency physicians in three states had little effect on the intensity of practice. Similarly, in another study on defensive medicine conducted by law and business school professors found that not only did malpractice reforms not reduce spending but also actually increased medical costs.

THERE ARE TOO MANY MEDICAL MALPRACTICE LAWSUITS

Some people think there are too many lawsuits in general and too many medical malpractice lawsuits in particular. Of course, the phrase "too many" involves a value judgment that is itself ambiguous: How many are too many? How is that number decided? What if lots of people are getting injured by medical negligence? What makes one lawsuit better than another? Let's look at the data.

First, in Illinois, 70 percent of all lawsuits in our courts are businesses suing businesses. Tort lawsuits, which include car accidents, slip and falls, and product injuries in addition to medical cases, make up only 6 percent of all lawsuits filed in the state.

AN EXAMPLE OF A BUSINESS VERSUS BUSINESS LAWSUIT IS ONE FILED IN EARLY 2014 BY VACUUM MANUFACTURER EURO-PRO OPERATING AGAINST DYSON OVER WHOSE VACUUM HAS THE GREATEST SUCKING POWER.

Second, in 1999, the Institute of Medicine published a report called *To Err Is Human* in which it noted that 98,000 people die every year because of preventable hospital errors. In 2010, the Office Inspector General for Health and Human Services increased that number to 180,000 patients, and they looked at only Medicare patients. In 2014, the *Journal of Patient Safety* published a study that estimated that between 210,000 and 440,000 patients endured some kind of preventable harm at hospitals, contributing to their death (and the authors claim these numbers substantially underestimated the actual rate of preventable injuries). To put these numbers in context, if the article is even close to being right, medical errors would be the third-leading cause of death in America behind heart disease and cancer.

Third, in 1990, Harvard medical researchers looked at a sample of 31,000 medical records and had them evaluated by practicing doctors and nurses to look for negligence. Only if two doctors working independently of each other concluded that there was negligence would the event be so characterized. The results showed that doctors injured one out of every twenty-five patients but that only 4 percent of these injured patients sued.

Are there too many medical malpractice lawsuits or too much negligence? I'll let you draw your own conclusion.

RELIGION

In addition to public policy reasons, another concern some of our clients have about filing lawsuits is religion. Whether it is wrong to sue your doctor according to your religious beliefs is obviously an issue no lawyer can answer for you, but it doesn't mean we don't have things to say on the topic. (What's new about that, huh?) What we have noticed is that, whenever this topic is raised by a client, the subject of accountability is often ignored. This is surprising because at least in the Judeo-Christian worldview, the call to accountability is clear: "What does the LORD require of you? To act justly and to love mercy and to walk humbly with your God." (Micah 6:8)

Ultimately, the choice between justice or mercy is an intensely personal one between you, God, and your family, but when making this choice, keep in mind that doctors buy liability insurance precisely because they recognize they may one day be negligent, hurt someone, and be held accountable. Also remember that accountability motivates the medical community to change bad habits and provides you and your family with compensation to help take care of those hurt by the doctor. This latter point is no small matter. If the doctor's insurance is not used to help those injured by the doctor's negligence, someone else's money will: yours, your family's, or, in catastrophic injury cases (brain or spine injuries), the taxpayers' money through public aid and similar assistance. In rare exceptions, neither of these two latter options can possibly provide the quality of care that damages in a lawsuit provide.

LIABILITY

If you decide that bringing a lawsuit isn't a bad thing, and if you bring your case to a qualified medical malpractice lawyer to evaluate, the first thing the lawyer will do is assess whether you have a viable case. This involves two main principles: liability and injury. On the liability question, the lawyer must assess whether the doctor (hospital, etc.) broke the rules of the doctor's profession. A positive answer doesn't automatically mean that you have a case, but without it, there is no point in bringing a lawsuit. To answer this question, the lawyer will do what I described earlier under the section on rules: the lawyer will research the medicine and talk to medical experts. What we cannot do is make up a case that isn't there.

INJURY

Even when a doctor breaks the rules of his profession, it doesn't mean that you should sue him. A second factor that a medical malpractice lawyer must evaluate is the extent of your injuries. Of course, any injury from medical negligence is serious stuff; yet, even with clear negligence, there may not be enough injury to justify a lawsuit. The reason is cost. Medical cases are very expensive. For example, it usually costs well over $150,000 to bring a medical case to trial. To justify investing this much money, there must be substantial injury.

Now, please don't try to decide on your own whether you have enough injury to justify a lawsuit. You are often the worst judge of this factor because your primary motive is to get better, and negative thoughts about your condition and its impact on your life often frustrate this goal. Instead, call a qualified medical malpractice lawyer, or better yet, have someone you trust and love who really knows you make that call. But understand this: if you think you should get millions just because the doctor forgot to call you, was rude, or gave you the wrong medicine, which thank God you caught in time, you're wasting your efforts. We get enough of those calls and I will tell you what I tell those people: be grateful that you're okay and find another doctor.

Let's summarize:

- The three most common factors in deciding whether to sue your medical care provider are public policies worries (i.e., tort reform), religious reasons, and the quality of the case (i.e., did the doctor break the rules and are you substantially hurt).

- The weight given these factors is up to you, of course, but make sure you think about the facts, not the propaganda.

- Injured people tend to minimize their injuries. Get an outside opinion before you decide that your injuries are "too small" to matter.

CHAPTER 3

HOW DOES A TRIAL WORK?

Most of you have seen legal shows like *The Good Wife*, *Law and Order*, or, if you are a wee bit older, *L.A. Law*, so let me start with the obvious: trials are not like what you see on TV. The reason is equally obvious: trials are unscripted live affairs with real people in real pain who don't have complete control over how events unfold. Plus there is the inconvenient thing called the law, which everyone must follow. Yet, I am hesitant to tell you to ignore everything you've seen in movies and television because all good trial lawyers know that the compelling drama that makes these shows so watchable is also critical in the courtroom. Thus, while I will start this chapter with the "mechanical" aspects of trial work, it is the second section—the "art" of trial work—that matters the most.

THE MECHANICS OF TRIAL

The parts of a trial are legal motions, jury selection, opening statements, plaintiff's evidence, defendant's evidence, jury instruction conference, closing arguments, and deliberations.

LEGAL MOTIONS

Before a trial starts, the judge will make legal rulings that affect a case. Every case has its own peculiarities, but let me give you a common example of a motion I raise before every surgery trial. Before surgery, patients often sign a consent form that contains, among other things, a description of the surgery or procedure, who is providing the medical care, the risks involved, and often, a whole list of things the hospitals or doctors say they won't be responsible for. Of course, except maybe in purely elective surgeries but probably not even those, no one actually reads these forms because there are no real alternatives if you disagree with something. What are you going to do? Take your emergency appendicitis to another hospital?

Now, many people think—and hospitals will never do anything to suggest otherwise—that signing these forms frees the hospital from accountably for anything bad that happens. This is not true. In fact, no one can ever consent to doctors or hospitals breaking the rules of medicine. Nonetheless, I can tell you that there isn't a trial I have been in where the defendants haven't wanted to whip out the consent form, wave it in front of the jury, and tell them that you consented to the bad things that happened to you. To prevent this from happening, we file a motion before the start of trial asking the judge to tell the defendants they can't do any such thing. These motions are called *motions in limine,* which is fancy Latin that means, "at the start of." Makes sense, doesn't it?

JURY SELECTION

The next stage of trial is picking the jurors who will decide your case. In my opinion, and the opinion of many good trial lawyers, this is the most important part of a jury trial. In its basics, it is talking to a group of possible jurors, asking them questions, and then approving some of them to be on your jury while disapproving others. In reality, however, there is an art to the practice that affects outcome more than any other factor. This art will be discussed in the next section. By the way, for those of you who have a thing for Latin, jury selection is called *verum dicere*, which oddly no lawyer ever uses. Instead, we use the Anglo-French phrase, *voir dire*. Don't ask me why.

OPENING STATEMENT

Following jury selection the trial starts with each side giving an opening statement. Once again, mechanically the idea is simple: each side tells the jury what they can expect to hear throughout the trial. But also, once again, the art of the opening statement is ever so much more important than the mechanics.

EVIDENCE

After opening statements, the parties put in their evidence by calling witnesses, showing documents, and demonstrating events. The plaintiff goes first, then each defendant. How the parties put in evidence is limited by the law and the trial lawyer's creativity. And guess what? Exactly! The art of presenting evidence is more important than the mechanics.

JURY INSTRUCTION CONFERENCE

After all of the evidence has been presented, but before closing arguments, the judge will meet with the lawyers outside the presence of the jury to discuss what instructions the jury will get. Jury instructions are literally the law that the jury is supposed to follow. These instructions are not written in plain English and, in fact, studies have shown that most jurors don't understand a word of what they read. That is why good trial lawyers reinterpret jury instructions into plain English during closing arguments.

CLOSING ARGUMENTS

After jury instructions have been drafted, the parties get to talk directly to the jurors for the third time during trial (the other two times were jury selection and opening statements). In closing arguments, lawyers are granted the greatest freedom to say what they want. It is here that the evidence is tied together and they ask for money. Mechanically, it is a simple process but, of course, doing it well requires … yes, a lot of art.

DELIBERATIONS

After closing arguments, the jury is locked in a room to decide who wins and, if they decide that the plaintiff wins, how much money is necessary to compensate the plaintiff for injuries. Any lawyer who actually tries cases for a living will tell you that this micro-intersection in time is the worst part of the whole trial because all control has been transferred to the jury. There is nothing left to say or do but await their decision. Yet, if we've done our part, picked a jury that cares, and went beyond the mechanics to the art, then we can rest knowing we've done our best.

THE ART OF TRIAL

The art of trial is turning the legal case into a compelling story. This means presenting the case as an entertaining event (which means interesting and enlightening, not necessarily joyful) without losing its meaning or purpose. The methods for doing this during the various aspects of a trial are too numerous and detailed to go through in a book like this, but because the art of trial is what distinguishes the journeyman lawyers from the stars, I want to at least give you the essence of what it means.

THE ART OF THE CASE STORY

I can go on and on about why "story" is so important to trial work, but the simple answer is that story is, and has been since creation, the way humans understand the world around them. Without story, events (and cases) are nothing more than a collection of facts, some of which may not even look related. Studies show that the need for story is so strong that, if lawyers present cases without one, juries will impose their own. Unfortunately, juror stories don't always match up with the point the lawyer is trying to make.

Thus, the most important step in the art of trial is to decide the story of the case. Most lawyers (myself included when I first started out) thought that the story of medical cases was about mistakes in medicine. But I was wrong. Take, for example, an orthopedic surgery case in which the surgeon tries a new technique to fix a busted shoulder but ends up with an awful result. The surgeon, and frankly too many plaintiff lawyers, will think the case story is about the right of surgeons to try new techniques. A lawyer practicing the art of trial, however, will understand that the case story is really about a doctor knowing his limits or about a patient's right to be fully informed about what her doctor is doing. Trust me, there is a big difference.

Finding what the case story is about is the lawyer's job, and we know of only one way to do it: by living with the client's case. This is not a metaphor or a symbolic statement. It is literal. It means doing whatever is necessary to feel the client's case the way its participants do. It may mean, for example, moving into the client's house for a night to help take care of the client's profoundly injured child. It may mean shadowing the hired expert in the emergency room for a night to sense the pressures. It may mean spending a couple of hours with a nurse friend to hear stories about the challenges of the job. In other words, a lawyer must do whatever it takes to see the world the way the people in the story do. This is not easy. Living with someone else's pain—even the pain of the person you are suing—is never easy, but any lawyer who refuses to do it, or cannot do it, is not equipped to handle medical malpractice cases.

THE ART OF JURY SELECTION

In what is a gross simplification, let me tell you about three basic types of jurors. The first is the juror who is biased against a plaintiff and will never change his or her mind no matter what the evidence shows. Consider, for example, if the goal of a trial was to get Mitt Romney elected president. Do you think you could win if the jury pool was made up of members of Barack Obama's political action committee? Of course not, and that is because your audience is biased in a way that cannot be altered. In medical malpractice cases there are always some and maybe many jurors who are biased against plaintiffs in this way.

The second type of juror is at the other end of the spectrum and is someone who comes to jury duty biased in favor of a plaintiff. Research shows that this juror is a rare species yet does exist. Of course, it is in your interest to choose this juror, but you can be sure that the defense will know who the juror is and work hard to keep him or her off.

The last type of juror is the most common in medical cases. This juror comes to jury duty with a clear bias against the plaintiff and in favor of doctors and nurses yet remains open-minded enough to change his or her mind. When selecting a jury, trial lawyers must, of course, identify juror one, the biased juror whose mind won't be changed and, once identified, excuse that juror from the panel. That is, either get this juror kicked off by the judge because of the bias or, if that won't work, use one of their side's free strikes to get rid of the biased juror. What lawyers cannot do is allow these jurors to get on the selected jury under the assumption he that they can somehow change the jurors' minds. They cannot. No one can.

But the real challenge of the trial lawyer is dealing with juror number three, the biased juror whose mind is changeable. With this juror there is only one way to succeed, and that is by creating a trust relationship so that the juror learns to trust what the trial lawyer says throughout trial. This important task is accomplished by creating an environment of openness during jury selection so that prospective jurors feel safe enough to be honest. But this, in turn, only happens if the lawyer is honest, and by honest I don't mean sincere and I don't mean nice. I mean honest, as in brutally honest. As in, if true, confessing our racial biases to make it okay for potential jurors to confess their racial biases against our black client. Or as in confessing that we think there should be stricter laws to prevent illegal immigrants from working in our country to give potential jurors who have the same bias against our illegal immigrant client a chance to tell us that safely.

Understand, I do not mean that a lawyer should pretend to have these biases to uncover those who do. Jurors as a group can always smell a rat, so pretending only makes things worse. What I mean is what I said. A lawyer must tell the jury the truth. Only if he tells the truth can he expect to get the same back from the jury pool. A lawyer used to lying, hiding bad facts, shading the evidence in the lawyer's favor, or doing anything that smacks of dishonesty will only serve to reinforce the bias the jury pool came in with—that is, that trial lawyers are lying scumbags. That kind of lawyer is almost sure to lose your case no matter its strengths.

If a lawyer has no biases—a rare and probably blind bird indeed—then the lawyer still must bring up these issues in a way that makes the jury feel safe. I have lots of biases and am generally honest about them, but there are times when too much confession makes people feel uncomfortable. When I sense that possibility, I use my family. (I get their permission first, at least most of the time.) We all have spouses or cousins or brothers who are biased and I simply tell the jury about them. I don't ever humiliate them, but I use their opinions as a basis on which to talk about the jury's opinions. But always, always, always, I am honest.

As I alluded to, the other benefit that comes from your lawyer telling the truth, not just in jury selection but at all points of the trial, is that the biased-but-changeable jurors see this and start to trust and believe what your lawyer has to say. Then, when the defense inevitably lies or tries to hide some truth, which it almost always does, the bias the juror came in with flips 180 degrees in your favor. This is because jurors believe those whom they can trust.

None of this is easy or natural and very few lawyers can do it. Being honest before a jury requires being vulnerable and admitting things that are shameful or look bad, and lawyers simply aren't trained to do this. Really, few people are. Being brutally honest, then, is an art, although it is one that can and should be practiced at home and in other environments so that, when lawyers stand in front of a jury, the honesty that comes out of their mouth is readily noticeable as being, well, honest.

THE ART OF THE OPENING STATEMENT

The opening statement is your lawyer's chance to tell the jury your story. It is also a chance to tell the jury the questions they will be answering based on that story. The technical name for telling the jury the questions they will need to answer is *framing.* Framing a legal case is an art. It requires creativity, experience, and, almost assuredly, some research (by focus groups and the like) to get at what the case is really about. A well-crafted frame allows only one answer (your answer) and forces the defendant to accept the same questions.

Framing is not lying. It is not crafting a question that your attorney likes best. Instead, good framing is always honest and always arises from the facts of your story. For example, I represented a little girl severely burned in an operating room (OR) fire. The hospital blamed the doctors and wanted to frame the question of the case as, Did the doctors make mistakes in fire prevention? Indeed, most plaintiff lawyers would have agreed with this frame.

However, operating room fires were happening across the country with increasing frequency no matter who the doctors were, and the reason was because doctors (and the OR nurses) were poorly trained in preventing fires. Moreover, hospitals were told over and over by the federal government and agencies such as the Joint Commission that their doctors and nurses were poorly trained in fire prevention, yet the hospitals were doing nothing to fix the problem. Thus, the question of the case wasn't if the doctors made mistakes (they surely did) but why they made them. Here was my frame: Did the hospital betray its duty to provide its patients, from whom they made great profits, a safe place to have surgery? Of course, the answer was yes.

THE ART OF PRESENTING EVIDENCE

Most trial lawyers think that presenting evidence is a science governed by the rules of evidence, but most lawyers would be wrong. Yes, trial lawyers must follow the rules of evidence, but how they follow they them is subject to much creativity. Take a simple example. I have a case in which a defendant doctor claims he successfully inserted a breathing tube into my client while she was conscious and sitting in a chair. According to medical experts, however, this story was impossible not only because of the patient's sitting position—the throat would be curved—but also because a conscious patient would gag and fight against having a stiff plastic tube shoved down her throat.

Now, one way I could present this evidence to a jury would be to have my experts use words to tell them what I just told you, and, indeed, this is how most lawyers would do it. A more creative lawyer, however, would go beyond words. Maybe he would use drawings or, with the help of his expert, create an animation. Or maybe he would act it out as the expert was testifying.

Imagine it. The lawyer starts by pulling a chair in front of the jury box and sitting the way the plaintiff was allegedly sitting. Then the lawyer would ask the expert to leave the stand and try to reenact the event for the jury. The expert walks slowly in front of the jury unwrapping the plastic tube in front of them so that they wouldn't miss its size and stiffness and then tells the lawyer to tilt his head back. The lawyer does so, and while in this position, the expert explains to the jury why sitting is a bad posture for inserting a breathing tube and moves the tube toward the lawyer's mouth telling him to open wide.

Would the judge let the expert actually stick a plastic tube down the lawyer's throat? No, probably not, but by the time the defense got its objections out, the expert would be standing over the trial lawyer tube in the ready. Do you think by then the jury would have any problem visualizing the event as if it were them in that chair? No way. That is the art of presenting evidence and is limited only by the creativity of the lawyer.

THE ART OF CLOSING

Closing is story time. It's when the lawyer weaves the story of the case with the law—the jury instructions—to answer the question the lawyer raised in the opening (the frame, remember?). Research shows that, by this time in the trial, some jurors will be leaning the plaintiff's way and others the defendant's way. It is here that the trial lawyer practicing the art of trial will answer the frame in a way that gives *his* jurors—those already agreeing with his story—a way of looking at the evidence that they can use to persuade other jurors. Make no mistake, during deliberations jurors spend time persuading other jurors to see their view or time being persuaded by others. A good trial lawyer aims to equip his jurors with ways to do the former.

Let's summarize:

- Putting on a trial has both a mechanical and an art side.

- The mechanical side of trials includes legal motions, jury selection, opening statements, plaintiff's evidence, defendant's evidence, jury instruction conference, closing arguments, and deliberations.

- The art side is turning the legal case into a compelling story.

- The most important part of the trial is the art side, and the most important part of the art side is discovering the story of the client's case.

CHAPTER 4

HOW DO I PICK A MEDICAL MALPRACTICE LAWYER?

Drive any interstate around your city or spend time performing Google searches, listening to the radio, or watching television and you are sure to come across advertisements from attorneys claiming to handle medical malpractice cases. Please, please, please, do not rely on this advertising. This is true for every law firm you find, including my own. The reason is that medical malpractice litigation is really complicated stuff that requires a lawyer who understands both the medicine and the trial work. Unfortunately, advertising is, at best, a limited snapshot of a law firm's abilities. At worst, however, lawyer advertising is downright misleading. I am sickened by attorney advertisements in which the lawyers claim to be experts in medical malpractice when these same lawyers never go to court, or they settle cases for pennies instead of dollars. You can be sure that the hospitals, doctors, defense attorneys, and insurance companies know who these lawyers are and so should you. The following are a few to look out for. (Later in this chapter I will also tell you the questions to ask to uncover these fake firms.)

THE REFERRAL-MILL FIRM

A *referral mill* is a law firm that advertises extensively for cases with words or images that leave the impression that its lawyers are experts in medical malpractice cases, but when you hire the firm, it immediately refers your case to other lawyers in town to handle the actual litigation. Why would lawyers spend money to get cases they won't handle? Because the ethics laws in Illinois and most other states allow these lawyers to get a referral fee from the lawyers to whom they refer your case. In other words, lawyers spend money to get your case because they make their money "selling" your case to another law firm without ever doing any work on it.

Why is this bad? Well, start by asking yourself how lawyers who don't actually handle medical cases can find the best medical attorney to sell your case to? Or ask yourself if you can really trust that they are choosing a lawyer for you based on how well such lawyers handle medical cases instead of how big a referral fee they're going to get. Look, it's not right, but some lawyers offer large referral fees to referral mills to get cases they're not experienced or skilled enough to get any other way. The point is, referral mills by design spend all of their time and money on marketing and maximizing referral fees, not on practicing law. Pick a lawyer, not a salesperson.

THE SETTLEMENT-MILL FIRM

Unlike referral mills, *settlement-mill law firms* actually do some legal work on your medical case but only to see if they can settle it. In other words, they are not trial lawyers and do not try cases. From the time they sign up your case they have one goal in mind: to settle the case as quickly as possible. Now, you may think that this is a good thing, but it's not. It's not because the single, most powerful driving force behind maximizing justice from medical providers is fear; I don't mean an irrational or manipulative fear, but the righteous fear that rises up inside medical providers at the thought of being held accountable by a jury of their peers. If the defendant's lawyers and insurance companies know that they will never face a jury because the law firm you hired is a settlement mill—and everyone in the medical malpractice world knows who these lawyers are—you will never get anything close to justice.

Think about it. It's simple psychology. When my daughters were little, my wife and I told them that cheating in school was a serious offense that would be seriously punished. So when one of them was caught cheating, we grounded her from trick-or-treating on Halloween. From her reaction you would have thought we were sending her to a super-max prison, but she never cheated again, that I know of. But what if she knew that no matter how much we hated cheating we would never punish it? Do you think she would stop? Of course not. It's the same with defense lawyers and the insurance companies that hire them. If they know your lawyer will never make them face a jury (e.g., miss out on Halloween), then why would they ever offer you a reasonable settlement?

But it gets worse. Because settlement mills by design place profitability over doing the right thing, your case is worked up on the cheap. Settlement mills hire the worst experts, send out boilerplate written discovery often having nothing to do with your case, take the wrong depositions, and do poorly on the depositions they do take. Why? Because litigating medical malpractice cases the right way takes not only takes experience but also a lot of time and money, none of which settlement mills want to spend.

So, with settlement mills you face a double-whammy: you get poor legal work and no trial. As a result, when you hire a settlement mill lawyer you never get paid what your case is worth. In fact, sometimes you don't get paid at all, and when *that* happens you're really in trouble because the settlement mill can't do anything else but dump your case. That's right. They call you up and say they aren't handling your case anymore and then you're on the street looking for a new lawyer with a case that has been worked up so badly that lawyers who actually know what they're doing often can't help you.

But even when the defendants do pay on cases filed by settlement mills, they only pay what is called *nuisance* value: a very small amount well below the true value of your case but enough to tempt your settlement-mill lawyer. (Earlier, I told you about another negative term called *short money*. To remind you, short money is a settlement for far less than your case is worth. Nuisance value and short money are interchangeable terms.)

NUISANCE VALUE IS THE AMOUNT OF MONEY A DEFENDANT PAYS TO GET RID OF YOUR CASE, WHICH THE DEFENDANT VIEWS AS A NUISANCE.

You may be wondering how settlement mills make money taking cases that result in nuisance money or no money at all. The answer is volume. They make up for small or nonexistent settlements by handling lots of cases. That is why, like referral mills, settlement-mill law firms are heavy advertisers. They need to sign up as many cases as they can. (Again, I am not saying that advertising is bad. I am only saying that it needs to be read and understood with care.)

One last point. I don't want you to finish reading this section on settlement mills thinking that lawyers who settle cases are bad lawyers or settlement mills. The fact is settlement is a good thing. It brings finality and quicker resolution than trials and is the result in the vast majority of cases filed. Good settlements, however, only occur when your lawyer knows what he's doing and makes the defendant fear facing his peers at trial.

THE DABBLERS

Many, many lawyers think that litigating and trying medical malpractice cases is no different than litigating an auto accident, slip and fall, or similar case and will tell you so. We call these lawyers *dabblers* because they only "dabble" in the occasional medical malpractice case that falls their way. They, in fact, have very little experience in working up medical cases and almost none in trying them. Dabblers aren't necessarily bad lawyers and may even come highly recommended by your friends. They just aren't the best lawyer for you. The problem with dabblers is that their lack of experience leads to missing information and getting taken advantage of by the more experienced defense lawyers they face. While dabblers mean well, try hard, and may even be very bright, they use your case to learn from, and the stakes are just too high to let that happen.

LAWYERS WHO KNOW THEY ARE DABBLERS BUT STILL WANT TO DO MEDICAL MALPRACTICE WORK HAVE TWO GOOD CHOICES: JOIN A LAW FIRM THAT DOES MEDICAL MALPRACTICE WORK TO LEARN THE RIGHT WAY OR ASSOCIATE WITH SUCH A LAW FIRM. OUR FIRM, FOR EXAMPLE, OFTEN ASSOCIATES WITH DABBLERS; THAT IS, WE FIGURE OUT AN ARRANGEMENT OF WORKING TOGETHER THAT DETERMINES WHAT THEY'RE ALLOWED TO DO AND HOW MUCH THEY'LL GET PAID BASED ON THEIR EXPERIENCE AND, OF COURSE, WITH YOUR CONSENT.

THE BUTT-KICKERS

In the show *Suits* (I know, I watch way too many legal shows), the lead character is a lawyer who never loses and uses this "fact" to get new clients or maintain the ones he has. Although at times entertaining, it is pure fiction. All lawyers, even the very best who have ever lived, lose cases. Any lawyers who tell you that they never lose are liars. Losing comes with the territory, and for those of us who care about what we do, it is immensely painful. Listen to how Gerry Spence (a very good and famous lawyer; think Karen Silkwood) described it: "I remember how painful my first loss in the courtroom was—watching a mother walk out of the courtroom with her young crippled son on crutches at her side. The jury had given nothing and had found in favor of the negligent railroad. Found against justice. Found that the boy could never be awarded the funds necessary to pay the medical bills for the operations he would need for many years. I wept."

Indeed, I, too, have cried after losses because they hurt terribly. In fact, every good trial lawyer I know has shed tears over a loss. Weeping may not seem strong, but a lawyer who does not or cannot feel deep hurt is not a good medical malpractice lawyer. There is no way anyone can ever ask a jury to feel something that the lawyer himself doesn't feel. And jurors will not help unless they can feel what the client feels. Feeling is the essence of the trial lawyer's job.

Yet, there are lawyers who will imply or frankly state that you should hire them because they are the superhero-tough, take-no-prisoners, shoot-first-and-ask-questions-later type of lawyer who will *show you the money*. Okay, well, good luck with that. We call these lawyers the *butt-kickers* and it isn't a compliment. They use tough words and an aggressive tone in their ads and in their meetings with potential clients, not because they're tougher or better than the rest of us (they're not) or because over-aggressiveness is necessary to succeed at medical malpractice litigation (it is not) but because they know that people who have suffered serious loss or death from medical malpractice are at their most vulnerable period of their lives, and talking tough often gives clients a sense that they're in control again.

And true enough, in the beginning, hiring a butt-kicker does supply a sense of control, a sense that the bad guys will finally get what they deserve. But it comes at a price. Like everyone else you know who brags a lot, the blustering behavior of butt-kickers hides a deeper insecurity about who they are. In other words, butt-kickers talk big to hide the fact that they're not very good lawyers. Yes, you will feel good at first, but when the inevitable bumps in the road occur, the tough words will ring hollow and all that will matter to you is why your lawyer cannot figure out a solution.

Now, before you get the wrong idea, let me state very clearly that quality medical malpractice lawyers are always tough. The difference, however, is that the toughness arises out of who they are, not what they say and always involves characteristics like perseverance, courage, and integrity.

OTHER THINGS TO LOOK OUT FOR

In addition to the lawyers described previously, there are other types of lawyers to watch out for when looking for a medical malpractice attorney. Here are some of their characteristics:

1. Lawyers whose ads claim they have a dozen or more "specialties." (Ask yourself, how that is possible, or how it is possible to be good at several specialties.)

2. Lawyers who won't let you leave their office without signing a fee contract. I discuss fee agreements in detail later in this book, but you should sign only after you feel comfortable. If that means taking the agreement home, then you get to take it home. If a lawyer won't let you take it home, beware.

3. Lawyers who call you first. That should never happen unless you've requested it through a friend or someone who knows the lawyer, which of course means you're expecting it. If you're not, ask yourself how they got your name and number. It won't be a good answer. It usually means they've paid someone for the information: a paramedic, nurse, hospital receptionist, someone.

4. Lawyers listed as medical malpractice lawyers in the Internet directories. Our law firm is listed on several Internet directories. Do you know how we got there? We paid for it. No one ever asked us about our experience. Use the directories to get a sense of who may be out there, but please do not rely on them. Always dig deeper. This is true even for the better directories such as Super Lawyers, Leading Lawyers, or Best Lawyers (in which we are also listed). While these are invitation-only directories based on results and reputation, they still shouldn't be used as a shortcut to doing the deeper homework I discuss below. (I know lawyers on these lists I would never hire.)

THINGS TO CONSIDER WHEN CHOOSING A MEDICAL MALPRACTICE LAW FIRM

I know from my trial work that it is never sufficient to point out the negatives—the things medical providers didn't do—without also showing the jury the good things the medical people might have done instead. So, let me list for you four factors you should look for—and ask directly about—in choosing a medical malpractice law firm. These questions will help you uncover the lawyers you shouldn't hire as well as the one you should.

SELECTIVITY

All law firms have limited resources—limited number of lawyers, limited number of staff, and limited amounts of money and hours—and it should be obvious that how much of these resources are spent on your case has a direct impact on how the case turns out. Of course, it's unreasonable to ask a lawyer to handle only your case, and such a lawyer would surely starve long before your case was over. On the other hand, it is legitimate to expect your lawyers to keep their caseload small enough so that your case gets the attention it needs and deserves. Typically, in the medical malpractice arena, this is in the range of fifteen to twenty cases per lawyer.

Aside from hiring more lawyers, the way quality law firms achieve this goal is by being selective about the cases they handle. Being selective means turning down even good liability cases if the damages are too small or turning down mega-damage cases if the liability is too weak. Being selective also means making the selection at the right time. It doesn't help the limited resource problem for a law firm to be selective after taking on a case. In other words, some law firms sign up as many cases as they can and only get selective after they commit resources to the case for a year or so. This strategy, however, results in all of their cases—even the quality ones—getting shorted of attention. Instead, the proper strategy is to screen cases at intake—that is, to spend time and money up front when the case first comes in the door to determine whether it should be kept. For this strategy to work, however, the lawyers need good judgment skills, an ability that only comes from experience, the next important characteristic of a quality medical malpractice lawyer.

EXPERIENCE

Many years ago—before law school—when I was a flight attendant for Continental Airlines, we had a saying that the "more gray in the pit, the safer the flight." What this meant was that the more flying experience there was in the cockpit, the more likely things would go well. This was especially true when the flight path was expected to be stormy because the veteran pilots had been through storms before. The same is true for doctors, car mechanics, electricians and any other professional you may hire: experience matters.

While classrooms and simulations (mock trials) can teach much about trial work, nothing teaches better than the time spent in the trenches. But, as I mentioned when I discussed the dabblers, experience is not just about how many years someone has been a lawyer or how many auto accident cases they've handled. The question to ask is, How much of the lawyer's work was devoted to medical malpractice litigation and for how many years has it been that way? By the way, you should ask this question even if cousin Billy swears by the lawyer because he helped him get a divorce. The lawyer may in fact be a great divorce lawyer but knows diddly about medical malpractice. Ask the questions.

EXPERTISE

Expertise is closely related to experience, but they are not the same. While experience brings much expertise, there are things law firms can do to deepen their expertise in medical litigation. For example, hiring a nurse paralegal to add some in-house medical expertise or, like our law firm, using lawyers who are also doctors or other kinds of medical professionals. Employing doctors or nurses is not, by any means, a requirement for being a quality medical malpractice law firm; however, having this additional expertise provides a distinct advantage over law firms that do not have it. For example, when I am preparing for a deposition of a defendant doctor, I have my partner Stan Heller, MD, at my disposal to work through any medical issues that arise. Law firms without a Stan Heller must either do without such help or hire an outside consultant to provide it. As good as outside consultants are, they never know the case like the in-house lawyer/doctor knows it, and they are not always available when needed. Plus, outside consultants cost money that ultimately you, the client, must pay.

PERSONAL ATTENTION

Giving clients the personal attention they deserve is a product of both case load and lawyer attitude. I discussed case load when I wrote about selectivity earlier. Now I want to address lawyer attitude. By far the most common complaint against lawyers is that they don't call or communicate. (The second most common complaint is about fees, a topic I discuss in Chapter 5.) Assuming lack of communication is not from handling too many cases or some kind of medical or work emergency (and that happens), then the failure to attend to a client is always about the lawyer's attitude. Let me say that again: it is always about a lawyer's attitude.

Too many lawyers view their clients as necessary evils to be dealt with only when necessary. This is wrong on so many levels. First, it makes for bad lawyering. As I have alluded to and said before in this book, the client is the case and the case is the client. Without knowing and connecting to the client, a lawyer cannot succeed. Second, lawyers are not—and listen to this—the ones in charge of the case. Yes, we have expertise and yes we need you to consider our judgments and recommendations in making decisions, but what we do is all about you, the client. At best, the case is handled as a team with the client. Although some clients don't want to be heavily involved because it is painful, the point is that you, not the lawyer, are the one entitled to make the decision about how much involvement you get. If the lawyer's attitude is that she is the one in charge, find another lawyer.

Let's summarize the basics for picking a medical malpractice lawyer:

1. Ask to speak with them, preferably in person. Don't rely on advertisements. And at minimum, review their websites.

2. Ask how many medical cases they have taken to trial. Get the names and case numbers of at least two of those cases. (Even if you don't actually check on them, it will make the lawyer think twice about exaggerating.)

3. Ask how many medical cases they have referred to other lawyers. Ask them why they would do that if they are experts in medical malpractice cases?

4. Ask what percentage of their cases are medical cases. Be wary if it is less than 10 percent as it shows a lack of experience.

5. Ask how many cases the firm is handling as a whole, then divide by the number of lawyers. If the number is greater than twenty, ask them how they manage so many cases per lawyer. (It may be that they don't handle a lot of medical cases and, thus, can handle more than twenty cases. But if that is the situation, then you have a different problem; one of experience—see question 4).

6. Ask them if they have any special expertise in medical cases.

7. Ask them who will be in charge of your case and who you can expect to get updates from. Will there be a paralegal assigned to help?

8. Ask them how they will learn about the injuries you've suffered. (Be concerned if they don't include spending lots of time with you.)

9. Ask if they return calls within twenty-four hours and meet with you at your request.

10. Ask them how much involvement you will have. Tell them if you want copies of pleadings, letters, e-mails, and depositions. Not everyone wants these things, but ask anyway and see how they react. If they tell you what you get, then walk away.

CHAPTER 5

HOW DO MEDICAL MALPRACTICE LAWYERS GET PAID?

Medical malpractice lawyers are *contingency fee* lawyers. This means that they don't get paid anything unless they get money from the defendant. In other words, the fee is contingent upon success. Although some politicians say "contingency fee lawyer" as if it is a cuss word, having such lawyers is a good thing for the vast majority of clients. The reason is money. With contingency fee agreements, clients don't pay anything—no fees, no expenses—until and unless there is a recovery. Hourly rates for lawyers with significant experience in medical malpractice is $750 to $1000 per hour, and on average it costs more than $100,000 in out-of-pocket money to bring a medical negligence case to trial. Very few clients—and I mean like none in my entire career—can afford to pay both fees and expenses to an attorney to pursue a medical malpractice case.

Further, under contingency agreements, if the case is lost, you never have to pay the lawyers for the time or money they spent. This is no small matter because, and there is no way to say this other than bluntly, medical cases are high-risk cases that are lost more often than won (although choosing an experienced law firm greatly increases your chances of success). Given this immense risk, contingent fee arrangements are the only way lawyers—and clients—can afford to pursue this kind of case. If not for contingent fee agreements, very few people could find a lawyer to represent them.

THE FEE AGREEMENT

Although many people come into our offices knowing generally about contingency arrangements—the "don't-pay-until-we-win" part is a prominent portion in lawyer advertisements—we've found there is still a lot of confusion about how it all shakes out in the end. We've found the best way to clear up the confusion is to explain the fee agreement with a hypothetical example of a case that settles for $900,000.

SETTLEMENTS OCCUR WHEN BOTH SIDES HAVE ENOUGH CONCERN ABOUT LOSING AND CAN AGREE ON THE VALUE OF THE CASE. THE DECISION TO SETTLE IS ALWAYS THE CLIENT'S. NEVER LET LAWYERS PRESSURE YOU INTO SETTLING OR TELL YOU THAT IT IS THEIR DECISION. ALSO, LAWYERS WHO FAIL TO COMMUNICATE A SETTLEMENT OFFER OR MAKE SETTLEMENT DECISIONS WITHOUT THE CLIENT'S CONSENT VIOLATE STATE ETHICS RULES AND CAN LOSE THEIR LICENSE. IT IS A SERIOUS THING.

HYPOTHETICAL SETTLEMENT

So, what happens after a settlement for $900,000?

First, the lawyers take their fee. The most common contingency percentage around the country is one-third, although it is not uncommon to see fees up to 50 percent. Some states, like Illinois, limit contingency fees to one-third or even less. Ask the lawyer you are interviewing if there are laws governing attorneys' contingency fees before you sign the agreement. Taking the attorney's fee—$300,000 or one-third of $900,000—out of our hypothetical settlement leaves $600,000.

Expenses are next. Earlier I mentioned that litigation expenses can generally be understood to be any money the lawyer spends to move the litigation forward. This is still true. The most common expenses in medical malpractice cases include, but are not limited to, court costs such as filing fees, expert and nonexpert witness fees, transcript costs (for deposition transcripts), copy and scanning costs (the most expensive usually being medical records), trial exhibits, medical research costs (retrieving textbooks and copies of medical articles), and out-of-state travel costs. Let's assume that at the time of settlement litigation, expenses in our hypothetical case totaled $50,000. This amount is deducted from the $600,000, leaving $550,000.

IN MEDICAL MALPRACTICE CASES, TRAVELING OUT OF STATE IS NOT UNCOMMON. UNFORTUNATELY, IT IS STILL TRUE THAT LOCAL DOCTORS ARE PRESSURED BY THEIR COLLEAGUES AND LOCAL HOSPITALS (WHERE THEY HOLD PRIVILEGES TO PRACTICE) TO NOT TESTIFY AGAINST ANOTHER LOCAL DOCTOR. WHILE IT IS NOT UNUSUAL FOR LOCAL DOCTORS TO WILLINGLY REVIEW A CASE AND EVEN STRONGLY CRITICIZE ANOTHER DOCTOR'S CONDUCT, THEY OFTEN REFUSE TO DO SO PUBLICALLY—THAT IS, IN COURT. CONSEQUENTLY, PLAINTIFFS FREQUENTLY MUST GO OUT OF STATE TO FIND EXPERTS WILLING TO PUBLICALLY TESTIFY. THIS, IN TURN, RESULTS IN MORE LITIGATION EXPENSE.

In most cases the deduction for expenses ends the deductions and the money that is left goes to the client; however, in an increasing number of cases, there may be insurance company and Medicare liens that must be paid.

Owing a lien means that if you recover money for medical bills paid by your health insurance company or Medicare for your medical-malpractice-caused injury, then you may have to pay back what was paid to you. Liens are a big enough topic that they get their own chapter, which comes next. For now, just know that they exist and can reduce your recovery.

That's it. That is how lawyers get paid. The only other thing you should know is that although signing a contingency fee contract with a lawyer is a serious business, contracts with lawyers are not like contracts to buy a car or a house. In those kinds of contracts, signing the contract means you may be forced to buy the car or house. With lawyers, the law will never force you to keep a lawyer you don't like. This means that you can fire your lawyer at any time. Just keep in mind that if you later collect money on your case, you may need to pay back this first lawyer's expenses and maybe even some fee for his time. Of course, if you hire the right lawyer, that lawyer should never give you a reason to fire him.

Let's summarize:

- Medical malpractice lawyers don't get paid a fee or get to recover their expenses unless and until they recover money.

- The first deduction out of any recovery is the attorney's fee, which is usually one-third of the recovery.

- The second deduction is litigation expenses.

- Sometimes insurance and Medicare have a lien for medical bills they paid that you will have to pay back. This is a third deduction.

- The law doesn't require you to keep a lawyer you don't like, even if you've signed a contract with him.

CHAPTER 6

WHAT DO I NEED TO KNOW ABOUT MEDICARE AND INSURANCE LIENS?

Whenever you get medical care, someone must pay for it. If you're lucky enough to have private insurance, then the insurance company pays for it. Otherwise, Medicare or public aid picks up the bill. If you recover any of the money they paid in a lawsuit against the person or company who caused your injuries, then you may have to pay these insurers back what they paid, or at least a significant portion of it. The technical name for the right to get their money back is *subrogation*, but you don't really need to know that. What you need to know is

1. Medicare and public aid have this right guaranteed as a matter of federal law;

2. private insurers only have this right if they put certain words in your health insurance contract; and

3. if they have the right to get their money back, then your lawyer must pay these insurers out of your

settlement before paying you (the technical name for this legal obligation is *lien rights*).

Let's look at these points a little closer.

MEDICARE AND PUBLIC AID—THE SUPER-LIENS

Whenever you recover for medical expenses paid by Medicare or public aid, Medicare and public aid have the right to get it back from you. This right is given to them by federal law, which means they don't have to tell you ahead of time, file anything with the court, put anything in writing, or do anything at all. They just have the right automatically. More importantly, this same federal law requires you and your lawyer to protect this right. What this means is that even if Medicare or public aid never say anything to you about owing money, you still have to ask them if you do. And if you do—they will search their database and give you a figure for the amount owed—you or your lawyer must then pay them out of your recovery. If no one pays them from your recovery and the money gets spent, then the both of you become personally responsible for the money from your general assets, even if those assets were bought with other money.

The lesson? These are serious liens that must be honored. Thankfully, the federal government recognizes that you had to pay an attorney to collect their money, and federal law permits these insurers to reduce the amount you owe by at least one-third.

PRIVATE INSURER LIENS

Private health insurance companies also get lien rights to your recovery, but the right is not automatic. Instead, they have to put language in your health insurance contract that says something like, "If you receive health services for personal injuries suffered as a result of a wrongful act, or omission, Acme Insurance Company has the right to recover from the wrongdoer Acme's cost of health services."

But even if the right language is in your health contract, the legal effect on your recovery depends on whether the insurance was provided by your employer or not. If it was provided by your employer, then the insurance company's right to get paid back is governed by a federal law called the Employee Retirement Income Security Act (ERISA), and if so, it is not a good thing for you.

Generally speaking, under ERISA you and your lawyer not only have to protect the insurer's right to recover its money (just like you did with Medicare and public aid) but also have to pay back every dime. In other words, under ERISA, the insurance companies get your lawyer's work for free; there are no reductions. This, of course, is not fair, but right now it's the law. Still, you need to know that there are several things that an insurance company must do to qualify as an ERISA plan, and these are things any experienced medical malpractice lawyer should know about and confirm before handing over any money.

On the other hand, if your health insurance plan doesn't qualify as an ERISA plan, then the insurance company's right to get paid back is governed by state law. Generally speaking, state laws are far more protective of you than they are of the insurance companies. In such cases, reductions and even a complete waiver of liens are not uncommon. Again, experienced medical malpractice lawyers will know their way around state lien laws.

Let's summarize:

- Whoever pays your medical bills has a right to get paid back for what they spent if you recover money from someone else. These are called *subrogation* rights.

- Their subrogation rights must be protected by you and your attorney. This right is called a *lien right.*

- Lien rights are serious business and must be paid out of any recovery.

- Often, your attorney can reduce the lien amount by at least one-third.

CHAPTER 7

HOW MUCH IS MY CASE WORTH?

The question of this chapter is one of the most common questions in a client's mind even if it is rarely asked aloud. It's rarely asked aloud because clients hear from the news and friends that people who sue doctors and hospitals are greedy, lotto-seeking, frivolous-filing, evil people who need to be stopped. And they think that this is how they will be characterized if they ask this question. So while they think it, they often don't speak it.

Regardless of what others think, however, the question is a legitimate one. In our civil system, money is the only thing clients can recover and is often the only difference between whether your family survives or thrives following the catastrophic injury or death of a loved one. Moreover, money is the only thing that a corporation like a hospital—which is not a person with feelings—understands. Thus, the question, what is my case worth, is perhaps the most significant question that a client can ask.

THE GET-RICH-QUICK MYTH

The first thing I need to do in answering this question is eliminate a favorite myth of the tort reformers: despite what you've heard, the court system is not some kind of lottery that helps people get rich. There are two serious problems with such a statement. First, every single client I have ever represented would, in a nanosecond, send back their settlement or verdict if it would undo the hurt that happened to them. Every one. The very idea that people file medical malpractice suits to get rich is an insult to everyone injured by the medical system. Second, the statistics say the opposite. The latest numbers are that plaintiffs in medical malpractice cases win less than 15 percent of the time and the amount they win is less than $250,000. So, if you think that you will be rich when your medical malpractice case is over, think again.

THE ELEMENTS OF CASE VALUE

Because specific case value is always impossible to pin down at the beginning of a case, the only thing I can tell you in this book about the value of your case—which I know nothing about—are the factors that influence value. The single greatest factor in case value is whether the "story" about what happened is a compelling one. To be a compelling story, your case must have the following elements: a likable protagonist, an unlikable opponent, and a loss a jury can do something about.

THE LIKABLE PROTAGONIST

The protagonists are, of course, the plaintiffs, and whether they are likable depends mostly on whether they are perceived as vulnerable. Vulnerable plaintiffs are critical because they bring forth the holy grail of emotions in litigation: empathy, or the ability to feel what the plaintiff feels. No juror ever votes in favor of a plaintiff without empathy. Vulnerability leads to empathy because everyone knows what it's like to feel vulnerable even if they haven't experienced the exact loss the plaintiff has experienced. Think about it. We've all had moments of vulnerability. Maybe it was a speech you had to give. Or maybe it was when your spouse had cancer and you let someone make meals for your family. Or maybe it was when you were out of work and someone paid your rent. The examples are endless because it is impossible to live in a relationship with other people without becoming vulnerable. (A great book on the topic of vulnerability and its importance in relationships is *Daring Greatly: How the Courage to Be Vulnerable Transforms the Way We Live, Love, Parent and Lead* by Brene Brown).

Vulnerability is most evident in people who are trying hard to overcome a serious loss but need help in doing so. They are literally laying themselves bare before the jury and saying here I am in all my weaknesses; will you help? (This is why being a plaintiff requires high amounts of courage. It's hard to be vulnerable.) Minor injuries, whininess, exaggeration, and anger are all examples of characteristics possessed by unlikable plaintiffs because these characteristics communicate the opposite of vulnerability. The more genuinely vulnerable the plaintiff, the more valuable the case.

THE UNLIKABLE OPPONENT

By *opponent* I mean, of course, the defendant—the person or entity being sued. By being unlikable, I do not mean that the opponent has to be Osama Bin Laden, although that wouldn't hurt, but only that the opponent acts in an uncaring way. A doctor who doesn't listen to a patient or return calls or a hospital that uses paramedics in triage because it's cheaper than using nurses are examples of uncaring, and therefore unlikable, defendants.

Doctor arrogance communicates indifference (another word for not caring). The reason this matters is because jury verdicts not only compensate plaintiffs for their injuries and loss but just as importantly communicate outrage to the community; that is, they are statements to the world that such conduct will not be tolerated. The more uncaring the defendant, the greater the outrage; the greater the outrage, the greater the verdict.

THE REMEDY

Last, case value is determined by whether the loss has a remedy. Except for the most biased jurors, juries want to fix an injustice. The more that money can be shown to help a plaintiff regain a normal life, the more a jury would compensate to fix it. This is why death cases are often worth less than permanent injury cases. Indeed, you may reasonably ask how juries can ever "remedy" death cases. Of course, they cannot in a literal sense, but with good lawyering, it is possible to create genuine empathy for the loss of a relationship that death causes—a very real but intangible loss.

Take, for example, the loss minor children experience when their father dies because of medical malpractice. In such a case, it is important to remind a jury just how important a father is to his children, especially girls. Fathers, for example, are in a unique position to model for their daughters how men should behave and treat women, and the father, more than the mother, has immense power to communicate just how valuable a daughter is. These are losses not based in greed, frivolity, or lottery-seeking behavior but in truth—truth about just how important fathers are and how vulnerable children are without them.

OUTSIDE FACTORS AFFECTING VALUE

Outside of the case itself, there are other factors that affect case value. The following factors are the three biggest ones:

1. *Statutory caps:* Many states, although not Illinois, have laws that cap the amount of damages a plaintiff can recover. These caps are artificial, one-sided (they only protect care providers), and unfair. Consider that if you seriously injure a doctor with your car in a state with caps, he can recover millions from you. If, however, he seriously injures you with his negligence, what he owes you is "capped" by your state legislature.

   The caps are especially harmful to the elderly, nonworking mothers, children, and the unemployed because their death or injury is not considered as serious as that which happens to someone earning an income. Usually this cap is $250,000 or less, and it is per patient, not per doctor, which means if more than one doctor is at fault for your injuries, they still won't pay more than $250,000 total. If you live in such a state, then your case is worth significantly less no matter how serious your injuries. To learn more about caps and to find out if your state has one, go here: http://ow.ly/X1tMW

2. *Poor lawyering:* As I've said repeatedly throughout this book, litigating medical malpractice cases requires exceptional lawyering. Without a good lawyer, you will not get the value your case deserves.

3. *Bad juries:* Earlier I discussed the importance of jury selection and everything I said there stands. However, what I implied with that discussion but now need to express directly is that the reason jury selection is so important is because the folks selected for jury duty have, as a whole, been heavily influenced by all of the rhetoric on how the civil justice system is broken. As a result, they come with strong biases against plaintiffs and in favor of doctors. Although there is much a skilled lawyer can do to reduce the bias, no lawyer can eliminate it. If your jury must be selected from a pool of particularly bad jurors (extremely biased), then there is a good chance it will reduce the value of your case and even perhaps lead to losing.

Let's summarize:

- What a case is worth is a very important question but difficult to answer at the start of a case.

- Value is based on a good story with a likable protagonist, an unlikable opponent, and a loss a jury can do something about.

- Factors outside of your case such as damage caps, bad lawyering, and bad jurors can reduce the value of your case.

CHAPTER 8

WILL MY CASE GO TO TRIAL?

The answer to this chapter's question is maybe. Statistics show that most personal injury cases settle, but as a general rule, medical cases (a type of personal injury case) settle less often than other types of cases. This is because defense lawyers and insurance companies know that jury pools have been heavily influenced by insurance company advertising and lobbying that says holding doctors accountable for not following the rules of their profession is somehow unfair to them or harmful to the public. There are many objective articles written about the myth of the medical malpractice crisis and I've mentioned a few in Chapter 2. But suffice it to say, these articles have not yet made inroads into people's attitudes and beliefs.

As such, there remains a significant chance of sitting a jury incapable of accepting an injured patient's message. This is true in all jurisdictions. For this reason alone, medical cases are more likely to go to trial because it greatly increases the chance for a defense victory. (This is also why it is important for trial lawyers to research, study, and apply methods for identifying jury bias during jury selection). Consequently, you should, from day one, prepare yourself to go to trial, and if you hire the right lawyer, he will make sure you're prepared if that day comes.

But—I can hear the objection—aren't the odds still in favor of settlement? Yes, and many lawyers will use those statistics to convince you that trial experience doesn't matter, but that is a lie. The Illinois State Medical Society insures more than 80 percent of the doctors in the State of Illinois, and it knows which lawyers can and will try cases and which won't. Lawyers willing and able to take a case to trial are far more likely to have a case settled for a favorable amount.

Let's summarize:

- While most injury cases settle, medical malpractice cases settle less often.
- All medical malpractice clients must be prepared to go to trial.
- Trial experience in medical malpractice cases is important for settlements as well as for trials.

CHAPTER 9

WHY HIRE US?

We've described and maybe you've even met some of the many medical malpractice lawyers who should not handle your case, and our hope is that, at minimum, this book will steer you clear of them. Of course you also know that it is our hope that you will take a close look at what we have to offer if you have a case that we handle. No, we don't take every case. In fact, we take very few. Not only must your doctor (hospital, nurse, or the like) have broken the rules, your injuries must be substantial. Trust me when I tell you that we reject hundreds of cases every month because there is either no negligence or limited injury. Believe it or not, sometimes people call about cases with no negligence *and* no injury. But, if your case meets our criteria, then there are several reasons why you should hire us.

First, we are extremely selective. This means our lawyers don't get bogged down and distracted by cases not worth our time. We don't believe in the "volume" approach of "little money on lots of cases." This approach never works in medical malpractice litigation and results only in poor legal work. To do medical malpractice right, each case must get the proper attention.

Second, we have medical expertise most law firms don't have. My partner, Stan Heller, graduated from Johns Hopkins medical school and worked many years as a board-certified cardiologist before going to law school with me at Northwestern. My other partner, James Harman, worked many years as a respiratory therapist before becoming a lawyer. Our *of counsel* lawyer—a lawyer who works with us on a consultant basis—Stu Perlman, is a board-certified neurologist. This is built-in expertise that allows us to understand the medicine better than others and to see what others miss.

Third, we're really nice people. Start by reading our profiles and checking out our photos and videos at our website: www.medsuit.com. We're pretty confident you'll find enough there to know that we are people you can get along with. We understand that no website or video can capture who we really are. The best way to do that is to meet us. Let us know and we can arrange just that.

Last, and probably most importantly, we're very successful at what we do. Following is just a sampling of some of the settlements and more significantly, some of the verdicts, that we have achieved. You'll see that with our experience and expertise we get results from all over the United States, not just our home base of Illinois. You will also see that many of the settlements are achieved mid-trial, which means, literally, after trial has started. Unfortunately, this is not uncommon. Many insurance companies pay top dollar only after a trial starts. They do this because they know there are many lawyers unwilling to try medical malpractice cases. We are not one of them.

DELAYED OR MISSED DIAGNOSIS

$8,200,000 Wrongful Death—Verdict (Illinois)

During a hospitalization, patients may get nutrition or medicine by way of tubes inserted into their arteries. It is imperative that these tubes be inserted and removed carefully so that air does not accidently enter the bloodstream. When air enters the blood, it is called an *air embolism.* If large enough, an air embolism will act like a beach ball that travels through the blood. If this beach ball—this air embolism—gets stuck in the wrong place, it can cause a heart attack. In this case, a major university hospital doctor negligently allowed an air embolism to enter the pulmonary artery. After the air embolism blocked blood flow to the lungs, the patient had difficulty breathing and an x-ray was taken. Unfortunately, the radiologist—a young resident—misread the x-ray, which clearly showed an air embolism. The patient, a father of three young children, died as a result of this careless removal of a central line and missed diagnosis.

$1,000,000 Wrongful Death—Midtrial Settlement (Illinois)

The reason cuts don't keep bleeding is because blood has something in it that makes it "clot," that is, something that is thick enough to stop the blood from flowing out. Clots, then, can be good things—when they seal off a leak. But sometimes clots form inside the body, inside a vein. When this happens, the clot is called a *thrombus.* If some or all of that clot moves to another area of the body, the clot is then called an *embolus.* Like an air embolus, a blood clot embolus can cause serious injury and death if it is big enough to lodge in the pulmonary artery. When it does that, it is called a *pulmonary embolism.*

There are certain risk factors commonly associated with the formation of pulmonary emboli. When these risk factors are present, doctors must take steps to prevent clots from forming. Some of the risks factors for internal clot formation include a close family member who has had a pulmonary embolism; blood clotting disorder; recent surgery; fractures to the hip or legs; standing or sitting still for long periods of time, such as on a long plane trip or car ride (the reason airlines like to get you walking); cancer; obesity; smoking; being older than 55 (although this factor has been questioned as of late); a history of a heart attack or stroke; and pregnancy, taking birth control pills, or taking estrogen replacement therapy.

In this case, a middle-aged man had been immobilized for several days following emergency surgery. The doctor rightfully ordered steps to prevent the formation of clots, but the nurses didn't follow his orders and the man died of a pulmonary embolism.

$750,000 Permanent Injury—Pretrial Settlement (Georgia)

In the previous case summary, we talked about blood clots leading to pulmonary embolism; however, blood clots can also cause another kind of injury: *compartment syndrome.* Compartment syndrome occurs when a clot blocks blood flow in and out of an area of the body, causing damage to that area. In this case, a young boy broke his arm, and the break led to a blood clot and compartment syndrome in the arm. Despite the clear signs, his doctors missed the syndrome, and the boy had to have the arm amputated.

DELAYED OR MISSED DIAGNOSIS OF CANCER

$7,250,000 Wrongful Death—Midtrial Settlement (Illinois)

Pap smears and mammograms are two routine and regular tests ordered to identify cancer in its early stages—when it is curable. When a doctor or hospital misreads pap smears or mammograms, the result can be catastrophic. In this case, a young mother of four children had a routine pap smear that was misread. She subsequently died after suffering a long, painful course with cervical cancer.

$4,000,000 Wrongful Death—Midtrial Settlement (Illinois)

Pap smears and mammograms are not the only kind of tests that can uncover cancer while it is curable. Even routine procedures such as hemorrhoidectomies—the surgical removal of hemorrhoids—can reveal important information. Any time tissue is removed from the body—tonsils, hemorrhoids, and so forth—the tissue is sent to a pathologist to look for signs of diseases such as cancer. In this case, a pathologist missed clear signs of a rare blood cancer that showed up in hemorrhoid tissue. As a result, a mother of three young children died.

DELAYED TREATMENT OR MISSED DIAGNOSIS OF INFECTION

$7,000,000 Wrongful Death—Verdict (Illinois)

$10,900,000 Brain Injury—Settlement (Illinois)

Bacterial meningitis is an infection of the brain lining and most commonly occurs in children. It is a deadly disease that must be treated as soon as it is suspected. If treated in a timely fashion, it is curable. Signs or symptoms of bacterial meningitis may include headache, nausea, fever, vomiting, sensitivity to light, and a painful neck. As a general matter, children don't get headaches very often, especially not severe headaches. Also, even very sick children will normally respond to touch or talk. So when a child comes to the hospital with a headache or is so lethargic that they barely respond to anyone, the people working at the hospital—the nurses and doctors—must think about bacterial meningitis.

In the first case listed earlier—one that had to go to trial and verdict—the hospital used an emergency room (ER) technician instead of a registered nurse in triage to evaluate a four-and-half year-old girl brought to the hospital with fever and severe headaches. Because of his lack of training and experience, the tech missed the little girl's stiff neck and light sensitivity and made her wait for treatment for almost five hours. The girl died in her father's arms seven hours later of a brain herniation.

In the second case, a two-year-old boy arrived in the emergency department with lethargy so bad that he didn't move even when the nurse took a rectal temperature. He also had a high fever and a stiff neck. At this hospital the triage was manned by a registered nurse who immediately and correctly thought "bacterial meningitis" and within minutes brought the child back to the emergency department treatment room where she told the ER nurse that the child "needed to be seen by a doctor right away." Sadly, the ER nurse didn't appreciate how sick the boy was and made him wait in the ER almost two hours before getting a doctor to see him (this happened despite having two ER doctors seeing patients with minor illnesses at the same time). After a cascade of other hospital errors, including an unwritten hospital policy that allowed the ER nurse to ignore a doctor's treatment orders, the little boy didn't get his antibiotics for almost ten hours after the triage nurse first said she was worried about bacterial meningitis.

$1,100,000 Wrongful Death—Settlement (Illinois)

Infections can occur in many different ways. Sometimes, an infection can gain a foothold in a surgical site. Hospitals and doctors know this and must look for it. In this case, a woman in her fifties developed a surgical site infection following back surgery. Despite constant fevers and pain, her doctors ignored the possibility of infection until it was too late. She died of overwhelming sepsis.

MEDICATION ERRORS

$5,000,000 Permanent Injury—Midtrial Settlement (Illinois)

Medications save lives. There is no doubt about it. But when used improperly, it can also cause serious injury. Too much, too often, or the wrong kind of medication can be toxic. In fact, medication error—especially in hospitals—is one of the most common causes of injury in a medical setting. In this case, the patient was given a drug to help with his arthritis. The drug was very powerful but well-known to be toxic to the kidneys if used for too long. To prevent such injury, the doctor is required to monitor the patient's kidney function while on the drug, and to stop the drug at the first sign of kidney problems. In this case, the doctor failed to monitor kidney function and the patient lost both kidneys.

$650,000 Wrongful Death—Pretrial Settlement (Georgia)

For many years, drug companies sold over-the-counter medications containing a drug called pseudoephedrine. About ten years ago, it was discovered that these medications not only didn't work in children under the age of two but also could be dangerous and deadly. In this case, despite all of the warnings about the use of pseudoephedrine in children under the age of two, the doctor prescribed the medication for a four-month-old baby. The baby died from the drug.

$500,000 Wrongful Death—Midtrial Settlement (Illinois)

This was another case of not monitoring the toxic effects of an arthritis drug. This one killed an elderly woman's liver and, ultimately, her.

HOSPITAL INJURIES

$14,000,000 Burn and Brain Injury—Pretrial Settlement (Illinois)

Avoidable hospital-related injuries are the third-leading cause of death in the United States. One hospital-related injury that is completely preventable is an operating room fire. Let me say that again: surgical or operating room fires are 100 percent preventable. Fire prevention is actually basic stuff that requires minimal medical expertise, but the key to prevention is making sure that every single person in the OR knows how to prevent them. Sadly, too many hospitals ignore this responsibility and let otherwise qualified doctors and nurses operate on patients without having a clue on how to make sure they don't start their patients on fire.

In this case, a surgical team started a one-month-old baby girl on fire. The fire was so bad that the baby lost her nose, thumbs, and fingertips and had a cardiac arrest when her breathing tube melted. The fire occurred because no one on the team understood how to use the alcohol-based skin preparation properly in an operation where enriched air was being used (air that has high levels of oxygen in it). Discovery revealed that the hospital had a policy of allowing doctors to perform surgeries without ever being tested or trained or otherwise proving that they knew how to prevent fires. Worse, although the hospital trained it nurses in fire prevention, it trained them wrong.

$2,500,000 Brain Injury—Mid-Trial Settlement (Florida)

After surgery, patients are brought to the recovery room. It is called the recovery room because it is the place where the patient recovers from the anesthesia. Basically, it is the place where the nurses and doctors watch the patients to make sure they wake up. In this case, the doctors failed to monitor the breathing of a forty-three-year old woman who was struggling to come out of her sedation. As a result, she was deprived of oxygen and suffered severe brain injury.

$1,250,000 Wrongful Death—Pretrial Settlement (Illinois)

A hospital has the duty to supply the equipment necessary to care for the patients it admits. This not only means having equipment that works right but also having the right equipment. In this case, a 75-year-old man had a blocked coronary artery (main artery that supplies blood to the heart). To fix it, the doctor needed a piece of equipment called a stent, which is a wire mesh tube that is used to prop open the artery while the blockage is cleaned out. This stent then stays in place to keep the artery nice and wide for a better flow of blood. In this case, the hospital did not stock the right sized stent, and it took four weeks to get the right size even though another hospital right down the block had plenty in stock to lend. While waiting for the right-sized stent, the patient died of a massive heart attack.

$975,000 Wrongful Death—Midtrial Settlement (Illinois)

Pain killers are important, but they are well known to have unpredictable effects and can inhibit breathing. This is almost never a problem if the patient's breathing is monitored and steps taken to correct any depression of breathing. In this case, a young man in his early twenties died from the effects of his pain killers after his nurse failed to check on him and then lied about it.

$900,000 Wrongful Death—Midtrial Settlement (Illinois)

Children and infections go together. Thankfully, most infections in children are minor and resolve on their own. Sometimes, however, an infection worsens and the child gets hospitalized for specialized treatment. While in the hospital, nurses and doctors are expected to monitor infected patients, especially children, to make sure they are breathing and properly hydrated. In this case, a four-year-old boy was hospitalized with a very curable infection; however, the nurses failed to monitor him and missed his increasing dehydration. He died as a result.

SURGICAL INJURIES

$5,157,000 Wrongful Death—Verdict (Illinois)

Procedures such as colonoscopies and endoscopies are routine and usually very safe. Sometimes, however, mistakes occur. In colonoscopies, for example, if the instrument is not inserted the right way, the doctor can perforate (punch a hole) in the colon or other body parts. When that happens, fecal matter, which is full of bacteria, can leak into the gut and cause severe infections. Consequently, doctors must be careful to fix any leaks they make. In this case, the patient's bowel was perforated during a routine colonoscopy. The doctor knew it but took way too long to fix it, and the patient, a middle-aged woman, was poisoned and died after much suffering.

$1,250,000 Wrongful Death—Pretrial Settlement (Illinois)

This was another case of a perforated bowel during a routine colonoscopy. Once again, the hole was not fixed, and the patient, a 75-year-old woman, died after much suffering.

$788,000 Permanent Injury—Verdict (Illinois)

Punching holes in the wrong parts with surgical instruments is not limited to colonoscopies or endoscopies. In this case, the patient's coronary artery was punctured during a routine angiogram. Because of the damage, the patient needed heart bypass surgery.

$409,089 Permanent Injury—Verdict (Illinois)

Once again, perforations with surgical instruments can be quite varied. In this case, the surgeon perforated the patient's bladder during a laparoscopic pelvic exam, leaving the patient with serious and painful injuries.

BIRTH INJURIES

$4,000,000 Brain Injury—Pretrial Settlement (Illinois)

After a mother goes into labor, doctors will monitor the baby's heart rate. This is called fetal heart rate monitoring. If the baby gets in trouble during labor—has trouble getting oxygen—the baby's heart rate will change. Doctors and nurses are trained to watch for these warning signs, and if they see them, they are required to get the baby out by caesarean section as fast as possible. In this case, the baby began to show signs of distress—she was being deprived of oxygen—but these signs were missed, delaying the baby's delivery. As a result, the baby was deprived of oxygen and suffered severe brain injury. Brain injuries like this are called cerebral palsy.

$2,500,000 Brain Injury—Pretrial Settlement (Georgia)

In many cases, newborns will be born with or develop yellow skin and yellow eyes. This condition is called jaundice, which is caused by a substance in the blood called bilirubin. Jaundice is very common in babies and usually goes away on its own. Occasionally, however, a baby is born with too much bilirubin (hyperbilirubinemia) or has problems getting rid of the bilirubin. If this substance is allowed to build up, it can cause severe brain damage (kernicterus). Getting rid of bilirubin, even in babies who have a hard time getting rid of it, is actually very easy, if the excess is promptly recognized. In this case, a little baby boy was born with too much bilirubin and could not clear it on his own. Unfortunately, his doctor failed to recognize the excess and didn't treat it until the boy suffered severe brain injury.

$2,000,000 Brain Injury—Pretrial Settlement (Arizona)

Pitocin is a drug doctors use to create contractions in a mother to speed up the birth of a baby. However, as usual, too much of a good thing is almost always bad. Too much Pitocin will cause the mother to have too many contractions; too many contractions will put a baby at risk by not providing enough oxygen time to breath between contractions. That is why doctors are required to monitor the baby closely whenever Pitocin is used. In this case, they didn't, and the baby girl was born with severe brain injury.

BRAIN INJURIES

$4,000,000 Brain Injury—Pretrial Settlement (Illinois)

Severe headaches should never be ignored. They can be signs of infection or something called a brain aneurysm (sometimes also called cerebral or intracranial aneurysm). A brain aneurysm is an abnormal bulging in one of the arteries of the brain. If you've ever blown up a long balloon, an aneurysm is like the bulge in the balloon when you first start to inflate it. This bulge is usually very thin and susceptible to leaking or breaking. When a brain aneurysm leaks, it causes severe headaches. If a doctor ignores severe headaches, the leak can grow and cause profound brain injury. A doctor diagnoses a brain aneurysm by a test called a magnetic resonance angiography (MRA), which takes a picture of the arteries in the brain. In this case, the patient came in with severe headaches and the doctor ordered an MRA, but the radiologist misread the MRA, which showed a very large and dangerous brain aneurysm. The brain aneurysm leaked and caused severe brain injury.

$1,750,000 Wrongful Death—Pretrial Settlement (Illinois)

This was another brain aneurysm case, except in this case, the doctor (radiologist) recognized the aneurysm but failed to communicate his findings for several days. The brain aneurysm ruptured and the patient, an elderly man, died.

CHAPTER 10

WHAT DO I DO NOW?

When we evaluate a case for potential medical malpractice, we start by talking directly to you about your story but, of course, we cannot stop there. We need to review your medical records. So, if you haven't done so, you should get a copy of your records. If this makes you uncomfortable, or you don't know how to do it, call us and we'll explain the process. Although in some cases we'll get the records for you, there are two reasons why we like clients to request their own records.

First, it means you're serious. In other words, taking the step of getting your own records means that what happened to you was serious enough and bad enough for you to want to do something about it. It means you're not just trying to use us to scare your doctor because you're angry at him.

The second reason we like you to get your own records is because a record request from a medical malpractice lawyer often does scare the doctor. And sometimes it scares the doctor badly enough that the harmful records will be changed or buried. I can tell you that everyone here has handled a case or two over the years in which the records we got after we filed a lawsuit were found changed from the records the client gave us when we were first contacted.

Generally speaking, you can expect to get your records within thirty days of submitting the request. If the provider needs longer, you must be given a written explanation for the delay with an estimated date of completion that cannot be longer than an additional thirty days. While the Health Insurance Portability and Accountability Act (HIPPA) gives you the right to obtain your records, it does allow the institution providing them to charge a fee to cover any labor, supplies, and postage involved in providing the records. There are also limited circumstances in which you can be denied access to your records. In this event the provider must put its reasons for denying you access to your records in writing, which you can use to have the decision reviewed by an independent third party._

Another thing you might need to do—and this is never easy but almost always critical—is order an autopsy. Yes, sometimes you may have to request an autopsy on your loved one. This is in part because hospitals do not routinely perform autopsies on patients who die while under their care. In fact, recent data suggests that autopsies are conducted on only 5 percent of hospital deaths.

Consequently, if you suspect that you are not being told the truth about how someone died (unfortunately far too common) or if no one seems to know how the person died, then you should get an autopsy. But make sure the autopsy is done by a pathologist not employed by the hospital. You do not want the hospital pathologists because there is a very good chance they are biased toward protecting the hospital and its doctors from liability and will twist the results, even if it's an unconscious bias. Instead, first try the county medical examiners, although you should know that they are not always willing to undertake autopsies in hospital cases unless there is something suspicious about them. If the county says no, then ask for a referral to an independent pathologist, or ask us. Even if you're from another state, we have a network of contacts that can help us find the right fit for you.

If you have to go private, the autopsy will cost anywhere from $500 to $3,000. Autopsies, however, are the most reliable means of finding out what happened in an unexpected death. Autopsies should take place as close to the death of an individual as possible, preferably within twenty-four hours to prevent organ deterioration. If possible, you want the autopsy to include toxicology tests.

FINAL WORD

What we at CH&H want most is to help you rebuild your life. Yes, we get paid for our work and in some years we get paid a lot, but no lawyer can succeed at medical malpractice law if they're only after the money. Judges and juries know it and, hell, even the lawyer knows it and the results will show it. Although imperfect as all human systems are, the court system exists to do good and that has to be the lawyer's first priority. If the lawyer you interview for your case isn't interested in feeling what you feel and in doing what is needed to make it right, then you should think twice about that lawyer.

Of course, as you know by now, holding a doctor or hospital accountable for what was done is not always possible. After hearing your story, we may tell you that you don't have a case. Please understand that this isn't a bad thing. Knowing what is true is always a good place to be, and even if you don't agree that it's good, it is still the right place and a place from which you can build again.

Finally, even if we tell you that you have a case, there are still no guarantees about how things will turn out. I know the butt-kicker lawyer will tell you differently, but he will be lying to you, something we will never do. Instead, here's what we do guarantee:

- You or your loved one will never be just a name in a medical record.
- You will be treated respectfully, kindly, and with compassion.
- You will be guided through the whole process from beginning to end.
- You will be kept as informed as you want to be.
- You will be given detailed advice about whether to settle or go to trial.
- You will be prepared and so will we if the case goes to trial.
- You will get the best trial any lawyer can give you.
- You will have a voice and be heard.

WA

Made in the USA
Las Vegas, NV
03 November 2022

58696717R00049